I
AM IN
CONTROL

—INSPIRATIONS FOR SELF-IMPROVEMENT—

GUS A. CAUGHMAN, MHR, MA

WESTBOW
PRESS®
A DIVISION OF THOMAS NELSON
& ZONDERVAN

WestBow Press books may be ordered through booksellers or by contacting:

WestBow Press
A Division of Thomas Nelson & Zondervan
1663 Liberty Drive
Bloomington, IN 47403
www.westbowpress.com
1 (866) 928-1240

ISBN: 978-1-9736-0039-8 (sc)
ISBN: 978-1-9736-0040-4 (e)

Library of Congress Control Number: 2017913342

Print information available on the last page.

WestBow Press rev. date: 09/20/2017

Contents

Acknowledgments

I'D LIKE TO recognize my counseling mentors and their review of this book, Dr. Charlotte Hamilton and Dr. Sharon Williams.

Foreword

THIS BOOK IS for those of you not born with platinum spoons in your mouths. It's a simple book to remind you that you are in control of yourself. Regardless of the situation, you have choices in how you want to live. Living successful and peaceful lives requires teamwork, whether it is with your spouse, your coworker, or your friends. It is significant to remember that the ultimate decision about your life's pleasures must come from you.

In life, other individuals will often try to sway your options for what's best for them and not you. Therefore, you must ensure that every decision you make is consistent and productive and aligns with your values.

A short synopsis of my story goes like this: Life was good! I had a great job working in a different location than where I live in South Carolina. On New Year's Eve, I returned from vacation and was admitted into the hospital two hours later. After spending forty-five consecutive days in the hospital with a diagnosis of multiple myeloma cancer and a tumor on my spine that prohibited me from walking, I immediately went through negative emotional instability (thoughts, feelings, and behaviors). The cancer and the immediate loss of my lower extremities doesn't make me an expert on emotional instability. However, I wanted to share my experiences, and I am a counselor who has years of experience in the field in this area. These are a couple of the many reasons why I wrote this book. Did I face adversity? You bet I did. It's a part of life. Adversity is when you are faced with difficult decisions or changes in life (death, jail, and loss of a loved one, divorce, bad news, mental and physical abuse).

While I worked as a counselor in a behavioral health setting, I had the opportunity to teach and discuss "life adversity" firsthand. After receiving positive feedback from several individuals, I decided to share these self-improvement concepts with everyone who has to make tough personal decisions. The ten statements in this book were written for you to reflect and provide guidance, if not for yourself, then for someone you care about. At the conclusion of each section is a takeaway. I encourage you to develop your own takeaways and put them into practice.

In this book, the most important thing to take away is that (1) spiritual belief, (2) emotional stability, and (3) physical capability, when equally met, will allow you to overcome any adversity. This is when you are truly in control of your life. If one level is not met, doubt in your abilities will occur.

There is no I in *team,* or is there?

THERE IS NO I in *team*. How many times have you heard that statement? Many folks have made that assumption before, but actually, I personally believe there is an I in *team*. A team's main objective is not only to compete but to *win*. In order to reach the team's goals, individuals have to rely on each other to pull their own weight. You have to rely on individual performances and understand how you fit within the team concept. Some experts refer to this concept as a "buy-in." You, the individual, are a significant part of the team. In order to coexist with teammates, you need to understand how you function as a person (what makes you mad, sad, and glad).

There are three major components the mind goes through when faced with a situation or processing a particular event. An individual's mind will think (T), feel (F), and display a type of action (A). Keep in mind that the brain doesn't process these in a particular order. It solely depends on the person because they may TFA, TAF, FAT, FTA, AFT, and ATF. The last one, AFT (action, feel, think), usually results in being apologetic for the action because you acted or reacted in a situation without thinking, and now you are feeling some type of way about your action(s).

When you are working in a team, you have to plan for setbacks. As an individual, you need to understand how you are made up internally, remembering that life does present obstacles. If you expect and plan for life's setbacks, then you can mentally, physically, and financially get through the event with minor delays. By not planning, individuals often place blame and want to hurt themselves or others. This temporary fix is not a long-term solution and will cause more harm than good in the long run.

By expecting setbacks, you have prepared yourself to say, "I can get over this because I expected this to happen! I can move on even though this happened to me!" You are able to move forward in life versus being stagnated. Listen, folks, the worst thing you can do is to fool yourself and not be real about what's really going in your life. Keep in mind that life is full of surprises, and you have to be ready for them. By knowing and understanding your abilities, you will not hamper yourself, others, or teammates. Together you should reach the ultimate objective of winning. Keep in mind that a team and teammates could consist of your spouse or a significant other. It's not limited to teams associated with sports or a job.

Takeaway

Planning for setbacks allows you to have an outlet even if there is turbulence in your journey.

Notes for Your Takeaway

_____
_____
_____
_____
_____
_____
_____
_____
_____
_____
_____
_____
_____
_____
_____
_____
_____
_____
_____
_____
_____
_____
_____
_____
_____
_____
_____
_____
_____
_____
_____
_____

2

Have confidence in yourself, and then do what needs to be done.

IT IS YOUR life—no one else's! You must believe that all things are possible. You must first understand what you want for your life and do what you have to do get there. You may wonder how others became successful. It's simple: you must have confidence in yourself and your abilities to get things done. Confidence plays a huge role in finding inner peace. It also allows you to think and make decisions in a clearer state of mind. Have you ever found yourself in a situation where you tried to achieve something, and it just wouldn't work? You possibly didn't believe enough in yourself, or you just didn't have the confidence. Ask yourself this: what is confidence? For each person, confidence is something different. To me, confidence is the ability to rise to the challenge, to know that you are capable of taking on whatever obstacle may be standing in your way. Confidence is not something we are born with but rather something we require, and anyone is capable of developing that characteristic.

Confidence is one of the most important traits a person can have. In my opinion, it really differentiates one person from another. I believe confidence leads to many positive outcomes that may happen in one's life. Some may believe it is luck; however, I assure you it is not.

Therefore, confidence brings inner peace once acquired. It works like a domino effect, once confidence is present, positive affirmations begin to arise, which in turn leads to your happiness which finally brings you to inner peace. For example, when applying for a job and there may be countless candidates applying for the same position; however, you may not have as much experience or as many qualifications in the field to fill that position. Ask yourself this: what would give me the advantage over the other applicants? The answer is simple, it is confidence. Confidence doesn't just show capability of doing the job, but it also shows a willingness to learn and grow. Once you get the job, happiness and self-fulfillment become evident. Confidence is built from within. Everything will work out if you truly believe in yourself and your capability to turn any dream into a reality.

Be positive, attract positivity, and never underestimate or restrict yourself from doing and achieving more. Always do what will make you grow and succeed; you never know who you're inspiring (a colleague, a family member, or a stranger). If you spread positive vibes, it will always allow the people around you to feel encouraged to do just as good or better. Confidence will always be that one factor that attracts any human being, regardless of what characteristic you feel you lack, whether it was beauty, brains, a great physique, and so on. Love yourself so that you will be capable of loving the people around you. You deserve nothing less than love, respect, and care as a human being. Anything else you need will be a bonus for you. You must first love yourself before you can fully and wholly love the people around you. Typically, as you succeed in life, so will others around you. Surround yourself with people who are doing good things and you will find yourself doing good things too. On the flip side, if you hang with bad people, you will find yourself doing less-than-desirable things. You are smart. Do the right thing!

Takeaway

Confidence is derived from within; you need to be true to yourself.

Notes for Your Takeaway

_____
_____
_____
_____
_____
_____
_____
_____
_____
_____
_____
_____
_____
_____
_____
_____
_____
_____
_____
_____
_____
_____
_____
_____
_____
_____
_____
_____
_____
_____
_____

Be happy with the reality you are in, not the dream you want.

LOOK AT YOUR life now, and find some positive aspects. Oftentimes individuals want to live like the Joneses and overlook the positive things happening to them at the moment. Don't be the one who dreams of becoming a millionaire but has no plan of how to become one. Instead of, "I should, I ought, or I might," change them to, "I will." Don't continue to purchase material things that create a false sense of security. This usually creates financial stress. You need to have a plan!

With privilege comes responsibility. Do not be selfish or cause suffering to individuals whose livelihood depends on your ability to make positive decisions. Credit card debt and borrowing from Peter to pay Paul are signs that you are living above your means. There is an easy correction; it is called a budget. Decrease what is going out, and focus on increasing your capital. Sometimes people think they are happiest when they acquire things. This is not correct. Remember that happiness involves loving and caring for others. It is annoying when people think happiness comes from receiving attention. This type of happiness often leads to depression, especially when you are no longer the focal point. Remember that you literally control your happiness and whether or not you feel depressed. Remember this simple statement: If you cannot change or influence it, or if it does not affect you directly, don't spend time worrying about it. It is okay to be concerned and caring, but if the decision is not for you to change, then accept it and move on.

I am not saying don't dream. I am saying that you must realize where you are in life. Making your dream a reality requires effective planning. It's highly important for you to realize where you are in the plan and to enjoy each step until you reach your goal. Don't say, "I want to be a millionaire," and start saving without freedom of enjoyment. If you have ten steps to get to a million dollars, then you should have at least ten things that you enjoy along the journey. Be happy with the reality or the life you are living. If you are reading this book, then I would say you are on the right path. Be able to distinguish false hope from positive dreams. Keep in mind that only you can determine your happiness, and your dream could turn into reality when planned properly.

Takeaway

Know what you want out of life. Write it down, and make a realistic plan.

Notes for Your Takeaway

_____
_____
_____
_____
_____
_____
_____
_____
_____
_____
_____
_____
_____
_____
_____
_____
_____
_____
_____
_____
_____
_____
_____
_____
_____
_____
_____
_____
_____
_____
_____
_____
_____
_____
_____

4

Do you have vision, or are you just being a fool?

MERRIAM-WEBSTER DEFINES A visionary as a person who has clear ideas about what should happen or be done in the future. That being said, you need to have a plan for what is to come next. Without it, you are like a blind person driving a sports car at a hundred miles per hour, racing through life without a purpose.

I believe people are born with the purpose of a higher power having a plan for them. It's your responsibility to figure out the plan. We all have talents to be great; don't waste them. I often see people at various ages rushing through life—for example, teenagers trying to be adults and young adults not listening to their parents, while thinking they have experience and know everything. Stop it, and act your age! Don't take shortcuts to achieve success—it is undoubtedly hard work that must be performed. The formula for success is to be passionate about where you want to be in life, have a plan, and strategize. Being confused and going through life without purpose often equates to wasting time. As we get older, unfavorable life choices such as drugs, jail, divorce, and so forth, occur and taint our vision. Much too often we get excited about our vision and share it with others who do not see or realize our potential. These individuals tend to cloud your vision with negative thoughts, which allows you to start doubting your own abilities. Sadly, this tends to get you off course. Traveling in the wrong direction makes it difficult to get back on the road.

People can experience some success without vision, but this success is usually temporary. People will begin to ask themselves: "What's next?" To experience full success, you have to realize a vision is more than a conceptual portrait. It's an exciting sensation that connects every part of your mind, body, and soul. When you are in the moment, it feels great. You see things clearer than ever, you're filled with enjoyment, and you have an everlasting hunger to continue. In essence, you have found your passion!

Looking back on life, I saw that I was happiest when I was able to help people. I always felt great and got a good night's sleep after helping someone get to a better place in life. Early in life I knew my vision was to be in the helping field. I planned and strategized to be successful. Today, I am continuing my vision as a counselor and writing this book for you. Everyone's vision is slightly different because people in general are different. Surround yourself with successful people, and you too will be successful. Hang around individuals who make excuses for life and you, too, will make excuses. Winners hang with winners, and losers hang with losers. If you want to get ahead in life, communicate and associate with people who are already successful at what you are trying to do. They will help you.

For you to be successful in life, you have to think strategically in the areas of family, happiness, career progression, and financial stability. It's simple: in life, take the necessary time to know where you are heading. Don't be a blind person behind a wheel of a sports car driving a hundred miles per hour.

Takeaway

Hard work does pay off! Reflection after completion makes one feel good about the accomplishment.

Notes for Your Takeaway

_____
_____
_____
_____
_____
_____
_____
_____
_____
_____
_____
_____
_____
_____
_____
_____
_____
_____
_____
_____
_____
_____
_____
_____
_____
_____
_____
_____
_____
_____
_____
_____

Peel back one layer, and stay true to yourself.

WHEN I WAS a teenager, I can remember being upset because I was not able to obtain the same things my peers had. Some students were driving to school, some wore expensive clothes and shoes, and others had the ability to drive home after sports practices. I wasn't jealous; I just wished I was in the position to do some of the same things. Shortly after high school, I began to realize there was more to life than those things that appeared so cool. I understand that things may look great on the outside, but internal issues are occurring simultaneously. Unwanted costs are associated with popularity, and like the iceberg, an abundance of issues often lie beneath the surface.

Let's face it—most people want the finer things in life. In some instances, the reason for the want is to show off to peers, family or friends. It's no secret that we want the good things that other people have (i.e., a good marriage, an awesome boyfriend or girlfriend, being accepted by others, popularity, and so forth). In trying to achieve these things, we often get out of our character that may result in financial instability, overspending and living outside of our means.

In life, you should never compare yourself to others. Even identical twins are different. It is so important—I mean really important—for you to understand that you are unique. The only person you should strive to be better than is the person you were the day before. Never compare yourself to others. Spend the time understanding your own self-worth. Don't feed into things that put you outside of your comfort zone. Although I wanted to acquire some of the things others had in my youth, it was awesome that I wasn't going down the road of being a follower. I will encourage you to believe in yourself and develop your own personal identity. If you ever take on the follower role, make sure you are following positive individuals. One day, you may become a leader.

Takeaway

Be you, not someone else.

Notes for Your Takeaway

_____
_____
_____
_____
_____
_____
_____
_____
_____
_____
_____
_____
_____
_____
_____
_____
_____
_____
_____
_____
_____
_____
_____
_____
_____
_____
_____
_____
_____
_____
_____

6

It's not about how you fall; it's about how you get up.

THERE WAS A couple married for twenty years who recently divorced. For different reasons, both felt their marriage had failed, not only for themselves but for their kids and immediate family. Their home went into foreclosure, and the husband had to file for bankruptcy. The wife felt she had no faith in her marriage. On one depressing evening, she went out with her friends and drank more than normal. On the way home, she got a DUI and stayed two nights in jail.

Their daughter was a junior at the local high school who was very popular but didn't win the homecoming crown. She felt worse after learning she would not be able to attend the prom that year because her family didn't have any money. Their son, a senior, broke his leg in a football game and also found out his scholarship would be canceled.

Hey! News flash! If you are human, you will experience disappointments in life. Remember that you are not alone, and it's probably not the last time you will face difficulties and challenges. In life, you have to juggle the good and the bad. Facing issues helps you build character and hopefully create a lesson learned from the issues or events. Remember, there are only two types of issues (the ones within your control and the ones outside of your control).

Issues Within Your Control

Is simply explained by avoiding common pitfalls. You should know your strengths, your weaknesses, what you're sensitive to, what puts you in a bad mood, and what makes you angry so you can avoid falling into pitfalls. Please, don't allow anyone to tear down your self-esteem. Stay in control of yourself. Depression is internally controlled by you. If you want to feel sad, happy, or glad, that's controlled internally. *Do not give your powers* to someone else. Now, if you are being abused verbally or physically, let the abuser know that if it continues, it will be reported or you will be prepared to leave the situation. The "I'm sorry" cycle will probably continue if the abuser doesn't get help. Sometimes the thing we care about the most is the thing that's pulling and keeping us down. They don't deserve that much focus. Don't be afraid of a fresh start.

Build on your accomplishments, and try to remain focused on the areas you like or feel the most comfortable with. Hint: If you are good at something, that's a strength. Take pride in the things that come easy to you and what you do best. In retrospect, avoid the things you are not so good in. "If you know you are not a runner, don't try to run a 10K. Just walk it and you will still get to the finish line." In other words, find other ways to accomplish what needs to be done. The great thing is, if you cannot figure it out alone, help is available. This is not the time to ask your family or best friend. Speak to or seek assistance from a professional whose only interest is to help you get into a better place and who will assist you with resolving your needs as well as getting you back up to your comfort level.

Not within Your Control

Some life events are out of your control—like breaking a leg or being judged by someone else. However, you are in control of your emotions and need to understand that not everything is going to go your way. Before getting upset at something, ask yourself, *Is this within my control or not?* If it is, then refer to the paragraph above. If not, then take the "stuff happens" approach and understand it's not the end of the world. If you don't win an event, just feel great that you had the capabilities and opportunity to partake in the event. Dealing with issues outside of your control may be the opportune time to consult with family members or friends; they will help you feel better. Keep in mind that nobody is perfect. Get your spirits up! Show everyone that you are tough and able to continue to grow from the disastrous moment.

You can recover from almost anything in life, but the only thing you cannot get back is *time*. Don't waste your time being apprehensive about things without value. Regardless of what happens, you can always recover from the situation. When it is done correctly, you will surpass the previous level.

Takeaway

Decide if it's within or not within your control. Know your strengths, and build, rely on, and improve them.

Notes for Your Takeaway

_____
_____
_____
_____
_____
_____
_____
_____
_____
_____
_____
_____
_____
_____
_____
_____
_____
_____
_____
_____
_____
_____
_____
_____
_____
_____
_____
_____
_____
_____
_____
_____

7

If you don't teach yourself healthy boundaries, then someone will set them for you.

BOUNDARIES, BOUNDARIES, BOUNDARIES … no, I am not referring to boundaries from a particular sporting event. I am referring to the boundaries that will help keep you stable in life. Boundaries can be defined as a circumference or a limit that is placed on something that will no longer be condoned. Basically, it's the zero tolerance you may have toward people and/or the zero tolerance you have for yourself toward particular issues. I believe both tolerance levels involve a basic test of our morals and ethics. When establishing healthy boundaries, it's important to have a line of determination that will not be crossed regardless of the situation. This may be defined as "developing a backbone."

When two people are involved, it is called a relationship. A relationship is between but not limited to couples, coworkers, subordinates, boyfriend and girlfriend, parents, and children. Within all relationships, healthy boundaries should be established. Poor or no boundaries in relationships usually result in some type of failure or being overly stressed about the issue. It's important for you to realize that without boundaries, *you have lost all control of yourself.* The other person you are communicating with basically owns you, your feelings, and your level of anxiety. If you cannot set your own boundaries, believe me, someone will set them for you. If you or someone you know continues to do unfavorable things, someone or something in the authority figure will step in and set your boundaries for you. In life, people develop habits. Good habits usually equate to healthy boundaries. Developing bad habits, such as stealing, may result in a judge and penal system officials setting your boundaries.

Three Simple Steps on How to Achieve Healthy Boundaries

First—*be honest with yourself.* Self-reflect on your life. No matter how difficult the issues were/are, you have to face reality and do what's in your best interest. Stop worrying about who you are going to hurt, and take your own feelings and your own anxiety level into account. You know your likes and dislikes—what feels good and what feels bad. Whose life we are talking about ... and don't forget that you only get one on earth! How do you know when you aren't being honest with yourself? It's easy. It's your intuition; listen to it. Since you don't have a crystal ball, it's best to be truthful with yourself; set small boundaries early; and strengthen them as your life progresses.

Second—*communicate your boundaries.* This is the time for one-on-one, honest, and serious communication, not a time for joking. Remember to turn off the television and radio. There should be no interruptions when communicating your boundaries. All distractions must be removed. Before meeting, write down the issues that need to be discussed so you can stay on course. Practice, practice, practice what you are going to say in the mirror. These boundaries will probably last forever, so don't take the conversation for granted. If the relationship is worth keeping, then practicing is worth the effort.

Third—*reinforce when boundaries are tested.* When your communication is completed and limits are set, it's possible that over time, your boundaries may be tested. You should be direct when restating your boundaries. Be nice but assertive about your parameters. Remind the individual how important your boundaries are to you, and make sure he or she understands them. Provide positive reinforcement when your boundaries are adhered to. For example, give a gift or simple acknowledgment. This should decrease the tested limits and create the behavior you are desiring. Now that you have surrounded yourself with healthy boundaries, don't forget to treat the individuals well, and the behavior will be reciprocated.

Takeaway

Decide if it's within or not within your control. Know your strengths, and build, rely on, and improve them.

Notes for Your Takeaway

_____
_____
_____
_____
_____
_____
_____
_____
_____
_____
_____
_____
_____
_____
_____
_____
_____
_____
_____
_____
_____
_____
_____
_____
_____
_____
_____
_____
_____
_____
_____

8

Do not confuse action with expectation; finish what you start.

ARE YOU A responsible parent to your children? Were you able to complete the things your significant other asked you to do? Much too often we get started on tasks but don't complete them. Some of us have goals in mind but don't exactly know how to reach them. Within this section, I want to remind you to stay focused on the tasks without procrastinating. We often get started on a task and it's moving in the right direction, but then we get complacent and don't finish. For example, I often hear people say, "I haven't had a cigarette in two days." This is a great start, but really ask yourself, "Is the goal for you to stop for two days, or is it to quit smoking entirely?"

Parents

You have parents who don't live under the same roof as their children. It's sad but a reality for some households. Some parents visit their children sporadically or annually, while others don't visit their children at all. Some parents, if they can remember their child's birthday, might actually call to wish them a happy birthday. I personally have an issue with parents who don't call and speak to their children daily or weekly. I feel some type of way when a parent states, "My child has everything he or she needs, because I am not behind in child support." I really hate the parents who don't provide any financial support. Hello! Childcare is expensive. You know the type of parents I am referring to in this section. And if this is you, I will help you out. First, it's important not to confuse activity with accomplishment. You are the reason why the child is in this world; finish what you started. Parent! Don't think providing money, calling once a month, or visiting once in two months is taking care of your child. For children, you have to spend a lot of *time* with them. Don't get me wrong; kids, like everyone, enjoy receiving presents. However by spending adequate time with your child, you are teaching him or her great habits, like how to be courteous, how to share, how to love, how to be safe, how to feel secure, and how to develop trust and confidence. The expectation for parents should not be the activity of providing things; the expectation should be to raise your offspring to become a man or a woman. Help your child reach his or her goals and future achievements.

Matrimony

"I love you.

"I love you more."

"No! I love you more."

This is how marriages start, but much too often divorce follows. Some couples don't make it to a year, while others get divorced after twenty years. For married couples, it's important not to confuse your actions with what's expected of you. It takes a lot of work to have a successful marriage. Couples must learn how to work together and coexist with each other as one unit. Many refer to this as "give and take" or a "compromise." Although there are many components that make a great marriage, today we are only going to briefly discuss family goals. In order to accurately finish what you started, married couples should develop goals together during premarital counseling. After marriage, individual actions on what you think is going to help the marriage will not work. You must consult with your spouse about your thoughts, and you can't be surprised if he or she says, "I would rather you not do that action, but improve in this action, for us to reach our goals together." These actions could involve but not be limited to the things that cause divorces, such as: abuse, addictions, communication, infidelity, and spending. Consulting with your spouse will decrease the time wasted and increase the chances of satisfying the family goal.

"I love you."

"I love you more."

"No! I love you more."

Basically, finish what you start … until death do us part.

Goals

Whether you are trying to accomplish your goal independently or with a family, the steps are the same. How can you accomplish your goal? It is simple. First, you need to identify the goal (task) that needs to be accomplished. Then you should develop a set of objectives (activities) that lead to completing the goal. Set areas of measurements to see if you are moving in the right direction. Don't make the objectives difficult. Last, plan for setbacks and recovery methods. Don't make it difficult. Start off with simple goals.

Here is an example of setting a simple goal.

Goal: Driving to the store. Objective 1: Locate the keys. Objective 2: Make sure there is gas in the vehicle. Objective 3: Get directions. Setbacks could be a wrong turn. Recovery methods are using GPS, phoning a friend, or calling the store you are driving to. Measurement: locate building or stores to ensure you are going in the right direction.

Takeaway

Keep in mind that all goals need objectives. If you do not have a way to measure your objectives, meeting your goal could be a challenge. When in a relationship, it's important to communicate with your partner prior to setting family goals.

Notes for Your Takeaway

9

Hang in there with faith and hope because you never know what tomorrow will bring!

"THIS HAS BEEN the worst month ever for me, and nothing is going right. Rent and car payments are due. I don't have enough money to pay for childcare, and I've been unemployed for the past three weeks. Since my brother's passing, I really don't have anyone to ask for help. When I woke up this morning, the first thing I asked myself was, *What's next?* Now I find myself on the side of the road with a flat tire. Will things ever get back to the way they used to be?"

Well, let me be the first to tell you that you are not alone. I say again: you are not alone. Thousands of people are experiencing similar problems, and seeing the end does often get cloudy. But the first thing I would say to you is to hang in there with faith and hope. You have been there before and recovered. Turn your negative energy into positive energy. Slow down, think, plan, and take action. Just remember, the key is to hang in there with faith and hope.

Faith is simply trusting in yourself to make the right decision. It's the foundation most of us were raised on. Do not take shortcuts, but believe that things will get better. Hope is when you see your future or anticipate what is going to happen to you. Having faith and hope helps you to remain calm during the storm so you can think straight and push through the horrific times you are experiencing. Have confidence in yourself and your abilities. Again, I would say that you have pulled through something similar, if not worse, before. Any time you feel you are tired and want to give up on everything, remember, there are several things you can do. Consult someone such as a family member or pastor. Talk to your best friend about your issues. Speak to a professional counselor, ask for a free session, and definitely continue after you find employment. You can check into the nearest hospital emergency room or call your physician.

What you should not do is to sit there alone, drink, smoke, or allow yourself to get more stressed or depressed. People are always there to help you, but sometimes you have to take to first step. Although we live in a world with millions of people around us, others do not know what you are thinking or what's going on with you. Take the first step. It can be beneficial if you are communicating with the right person. Try to separate your issues and find potential solutions for each one. If you are trying to work through multiple issues, this can be overbearing. Try to prioritize and rank them, and work on the most dreadful for you first. If it's financial, as in the examples above, call the creditor. Most of the time, they will work with you through this horrendous time. Good luck, and remember to have faith and hope.

Takeaway

Don't go through this phase alone. Help is there. But be prepared because it may take time for your life to change, but you will pull through the adversity.

Notes for Your Takeaway

_____
_____
_____
_____
_____
_____
_____
_____
_____
_____
_____
_____
_____
_____
_____
_____
_____
_____
_____
_____
_____
_____
_____
_____
_____
_____
_____
_____
_____
_____
_____
_____
_____

10

If it's worth having, it's worth working and waiting for.

ONE TERRIBLE THING in life is that some people want everything now. Rarely do they want to work hard to acquire the things that often take time to achieve. I know you've heard the saying, "I need to win the lottery! Yes, I am playing my favorite numbers." Really! It's important to (1) wait patiently and work hard for your happiness and (2) seriously distinguish between your wants and your needs.

Have you ever gotten paid on Friday and been broke by the following Monday? Have you ever purchased something you found out later that you really didn't need? Did you marry too early or maybe the wrong person for the wrong reasons? Astonishing, right? But there are married individuals who have doubts about their spouses. I won't discuss divorce in grave detail, but it often deals with moving too or communication fallacies. A way to avoid divorce is to take ample time in the beginning and date your mate. A great relationship takes time to build. If it's worth having, it's worth waiting and working for. Be careful not to rush into something you might regret later. In most cases, ample time will let you know if you made the right decision. If you decide to rush or move fast, then don't blame anyone for the outcome. Take ownership if you are the cause and hopefully things will work in your favor when it's concluded.

Promotion is always a sticky subject to discuss. Although we see the benefit in moving up in the company or organization, we also need to evaluate ourselves to make sure that we are ready for the increased responsibility. You have seen it before when people get promoted too early and the job is too much for them to handle. It is essential to remember that as accountability increases, so does pressure. If you are not careful, you can find yourself leading to false perception and/or disappointment.

Take your time in whatever you are currently doing in life; don't rush. You should enjoy the journey at each stage. I know life is short, but that doesn't mean you have to have everything now. You can substitute anything (buying a car, having a baby, or changing schools) for what I am talking about. There are always more events surrounding the main topic. Take your time and evaluate the entire issue before making your decisions. If it's worth having, it's worth waiting until you are truly ready for it.

Takeaway

Maybe the thing you are striving for might not be good for you. Evaluate and seriously consider if you are ready for the next step. Don't rush, prepare, and organize yourself. If it is meant to be, then in time you will receive it.

Notes for Your Takeaway

Bibliography

"THE RELATIONSHIP BETWEEN inner confidence and peace," Accessed July 21, 2016; *Kuwait Times* http://news.kuwaittimes.net/website/the-relation-between-confidence-and-inner-peace/

Merriam-Webster Dictionary online, Accessed July 21, 2016; https://www.merriam-webster.com/

About the Author

GUS A. CAUGHMAN is a retired United States Air Force veteran who served in Operation Iraqi Freedom. He counseled service members and their families on personal issues for 11 continuous years and worked in numerous behavioral health settings after retirement. Gus received dual Master's degrees (Human Relations from Oklahoma University and Clinical Mental Health Counseling from South University). He is currently the owner of the private organization, Caughman Cares.

Printed in the United States
By Bookmasters